The Diva Diaries™ Devotionals

RUTH: IN THE RIGHT FIELD

The Diva Diaries™ Devotionals

RUTH: IN THE RIGHT FIELD

Crystal-Marie Mitchell

The Diva Inc.
thedivainc.com
info@thedivainc.com

The Diva Diaries™ Devotionals Ruth: In The Right Field

Cover & Interior Design: Crystal-Marie Mitchell | IsrylDesigns | isryl@isryldesigns.com
Images: pexels.com Used under the Creative Commons Zero License
Author Picture: Ira Willis
Published by: CreateSpace Independent Publishing Platform, North Charleston, SC

Printed in the United States of America

All my love...

It is with great pleasure that I present to you my first devotional titled, The Diva Diaries™ Devotionals Ruth: In The Right Field. I started writing this devotional for two reasons: First, I wanted to dig deeper into the Word of God and two, I want to use this as a way to share my purpose + gifts with you. It took me a while to realize that everything I have been through in life and will go through is not just a lesson for me, it's a lesson for the people that I am supposed to reach and encourage.

I want to, first, thank God for breathing this into my spirit. I studied the book of Ruth, in the Bible, for weeks and wrote down the fundamentals of this devotional in one night after being inspired by what the Holy Spirit was revealing to me. I've heard the story of Ruth preached many times and have read it many times as well, but I wanted to explore it further as I prepare for my Boaz.

Thank you, Randall Clark Leichti, for confirming to me that I was supposed to write a devotional. You have no idea how God used you. I know we discussed a 30-day devotional and that is coming soon. This one had to come first. I appreciate you, my friend, for staying in touch throughout the years and reminding me that God sends people into our lives for great purposes.

I want to especially thank my Dad. As I am writing about Boaz, I am reminded of your sacrifices for mom and I, and what it looks like to be a man who puts his wife and family first. Thank you.

To Lady Meredith, my launch team and my DCF family, I love and appreciate you.

Crystal-Marie

Inside

Inside...

Forward

Forward...

Proverbs 18:22 states, *"He who finds a wife finds what is good and receives favor from the Lord."*

As women of faith, we have all experienced our fair share of life's seasons...some we treasure, and others we care to forget, especially in our pursuit of true love.

In The Diva Diaries™ Devotionals Ruth: In The Right Field, author Crystal-Marie Mitchell offers us her perspective on the journey of Ruth who experienced loss and sacrifice as well as the love of Boaz, the man God sent to her.

Through this reflective devotional, Crystal-Marie encourages us to explore our areas of challenges and opportunities in order to move towards self-improvement, self-love, and internal joy and peace as we wait for our Boaz.

This devotional supports Crystal-Marie's commitment to her ministry of healing and empowerment for women.

Personal. Inspiring. Heartfelt.

Dr. Judith Ned

Introduction

Introduction...

Do you find yourself in a season of singleness where you are preparing for your mate? How are you preparing?

These are the questions I've found myself confronting in this season of life. I've also had to shift my focus to God first before seeking out a relationship. God has a way of getting our attention when we are not as focused on Him as we should be. He had to shift my focus so that I can walk into my purpose and be in position to carry out His will over mine.

I've been praying that God would help me to prepare for my husband. That prayer led me to studying Ruth and writing this devotional. Am I the only one who is praying that God would give clarity as I pursue the desires of my heart? I believe there are others who share this prayer. So, I thought I would share with you what I've gleaned from my study.

This is a four-week study and each chapter is meant to help you dig deeper into the Word of God and survey yourself as you prepare for your mate. Each chapter has questions for you to answer as well as exercise(s) to complete that will help you self-reflect.

In this study, you will learn:
- That God may have to shake your life up to get your attention
- What a covenant friend/partner is and why this is important to your growth.
- What you should be doing in the wait for your Boaz.
- How being in the *right* relationship is better than just being in any relationship

Let's dig deeper together...

Ruth Week 1

Ruth: Week One.

Read Ruth Chapter 1

What a story! Naomi and her family decided to leave one issue - the famine - only to experience another years later - the death of her husband and sons. I imagine Naomi to have gotten comfortable with her new life in Moab. She had, for all we know, lived a blessed life with her husband, two sons, and her daughters-in-law.

I remember celebrating my birthday one year. It was a time where I was happy and content. I had previously experienced some hardships but nothing like what I was about to go through. That birthday, I received a message from an old friend from college. I didn't think much of it at first. But months later we were in love. Well at least, I thought we were. I ignored many red flags in our relationship and God had to use that relationship and its ending to reset my path (Romans 8:28). Luckily, every poor decision I made at the time, God not only forgave but He used for my good. But when I look back at all I went through, I wish I had made better decisions and was stronger in my faith. I had gotten comfortable and content and that is when the enemy presented me with something I wanted deeply–love. It wasn't true love and it wasn't blessed by God. God had allowed me to uproot myself from where I lived and move to be with my "love." God allowed it but it wasn't His will. When it fell apart, God wanted to know if I could focus on Him now. He allowed me to be shaken to the core over this relationship so that He could shift my focus from concentrating on having a man's love to basking in His love–the ultimate love. A love that redeems and not destroys. A love that is true and not false. A love that is everlasting not seasonal or convenient.

There have been a few more times than I would like to admit where God has had to drastically shake up my life to get my attention. I hear you now, Lord! That's why I've called my current season the "Get it Right" season. I don't want to get it wrong anymore. It's God's way or no way!

What I've also found is that when you truly get into your *Get it Right* season God will place those people in your life that will help strengthen your resolve, pray for you and rejoice with you about God's blessings on your life - covenant people. People who are meant to stay in your life through valleys and mountain tops.

In my book, The Diva Diaries™ Living Through Tough Seasons, I describe covenant people as Lifetime people. People who are with you through life's twists and turns, ups and downs, happy times and sad times. I also love the way Van Moody describes a covenant parter in his book, The People Factor:

A covenant partner is mature in faith and will remind you that God is faithful, that His Word is true, and that He never, ever fails.

I've been blessed in my life to have some AMAZING friends. Two of my oldest friends are people who have seen the good, the bad and the extremely ugly. And they have NEVER wavered. We all met in high school and somewhere around our senior year, we became close and became BFFs. Our friendship has survived distance, life, seasons and many, many, many downs. Its easy for the most part, for a friendship to survive the ups. But, its the downs that truly let you know if you have covenant partners. I remember one of my BFFs telling me I needed therapy and the other told me years ago that I need to "get on my knees before God." Both pieces of advice came during times I was so down I didn't' know if I was going to make it to the next day. See, your covenant partners are not there just to praise you and rejoice with you when times are good. They also have to love you enough to tell you the truth (Proverbs 27:6).

Ruth was a covenant partner to Naomi. Although Naomi told her to return to her home and her gods, Ruth clung tightly to Naomi (Ruth 1:16). Naomi had no more sons for her to marry, no more income and, for the most part, Naomi had lost everything. She even lost some of her faith when she changed her name to Mara (Ruth 1:20).

Why do we do that to ourselves? We tell ourselves that we are unworthy of this or that. Unworthy of love. Unworthy of wealth. Unworthy to be used by God. We think that God has forgotten about us. But He hasn't. And He didn't call us unworthy. It is EXACTLY because of the messes we have made that He can use us so greatly. "He didn't call the equipped, He equipped the called." Not sure who said this first, but it is true.

All he needs us to do is be willing vessels that can be used for His glory. So there is no need to change your name because of your past failures. God has given you the gift of forgiveness. He has passed along his Grace and Mercy so that you no longer feel you have to "change your name" because of a difficult situation. Take a moment to thank God for your covenant partners. Thank you Jesus!

Have you ever gotten so comfortable with your life that God had to shake things up to get your attention? What happened and what was God trying to tell or teach you?

_____
_____
_____
_____
_____
_____

Identify your covenant partners? How are they reminding you that God is faithful through the tough seasons in your life?

_____
_____
_____
_____
_____

Have you ever looked at your situation or past sins, as Naomi did, and felt you were unworthy? What does God's Word say about you?

_____
_____
_____
_____
_____

Prayer...

Lord God,

Thank you for shaking up my life and calling me closer to you. Thank you for placing people in my life who are to be covenant partners with me. Please give me discernment as you bring people into my life on whether they are there for a reason, season or lifetime. Thank you for forgiving my sins and staying with me through all of my storms. I love you, Lord, and I appreciate you.

Amen.

COMPLETE EXERCISE ONE ON PAGES 39 & 40

What I'm Gleaning...

Ruth: Week Two.

Read Ruth Chapter 2

I love how Ruth was living her life and moved on in spite of what looked like a depressing situation. She was in a new land with no money and only her mother-in-law. This was in a time when it was critical to have a male relative around. But Ruth didn't seem to care. She was set to do what had to be done. I admire her. I want to be liker her in this way. But if I'm honest with you, there have been times that I've let rough situations pull me into deep depression and upset peace. But what did Ruth do? She went to work (Ruth 2:2). Many times we are often preoccupied thinking about the things that we want - love - that we forget the things we have during singleness - time being the most important. Yes, I know, I am with you sister. I want to be married too. But when I look at all my married friends and how they cannot just go somewhere on a whim or start a business without carefully considering how it affects their family, I am grateful for my season of singleness.

What work are you doing while waiting for Boaz?

_____

_____

_____

_____

_____

_____

In my single season after a rough breakup, I published my first book, The Diva Diaries™ Living Through Tough Seasons. If I had stayed in that relationship - the wrong relationship - I would not have likely written that book or this devotional. So, where is your focus sister? Are you still worried that you won't find Mr. Right or are you focused on achieving the dreams that God has for you to achieve during your single season? God will give you the desires of your heart. But if you are always focused on what you lack you will always be lacking.

Besides career, there are many other things we should be working on while single. #everyheartmatters #heartcheck Singleness is a great time to learn to let go of unnecessary "junk" in your heart. Do you have daddy issues? Mommy issues? Past relationship issues that you need to give to God? This is the time to get your heart in order (Proverbs 4:23).

Who do you need to forgive or ask forgiveness from? Before we can get our Boaz, we need to make sure there is space and a clear slate for him when he gets here.

#healthydiva #fitdiva We had a guest preacher at my church who was speaking about our "Due Season." She spoke on preparing for what we want and living in expectation. She asked for those of us who want to be married to stand and then she asked do we look the way we want to look. I'll be honest and say that I have about 50 extra pounds that need to disappear. Not for Boaz, but for me! I'm sure he will appreciate it when he comes but, I don't want to wait until he is here to lose the weight. And once he comes, I may not have time anyway.

While Ruth was working in the field Boaz asked about her. He then instructs his men not to harm her (Ruth 2:9) and lets her know that she should stay in *his* field (Ruth 2:8). Wow! He protects her! When I look back on some of the relationships that I've had (while not physically abusive), I can say that I wouldn't describe my exes as Boaz. They weren't protectors - at least not of me.

Survey your past relationships. Would you describe your ex or exes as protectors? Did he/they protect your heart? Your goals? Your body?

_____
_____
_____
_____
_____
_____

The more we learn and grow in Christ, the more He will direct our paths. His will for our lives will become our will. The only way Ruth could be protected by Boaz was because she was in *his* field.

I know you are probably asking how Ruth knew to go to the right field. I know you are saying she was lucky. But there is no luck with God. Only purpose and God's plan (Jeremiah 29:11). When you are walking closely with God, He will place you in the right field, using the Holy Spirit to guide you there.

What have you learned from the way that Boaz treated Ruth in Chapter 2 that you will carry into your next relationship? How many times have you been in the wrong field (relationship)? What was it that kept you there? Loneliness? Desperation?

_____
_____
_____
_____
_____
_____
_____
_____
_____
_____
_____
_____
_____
_____
_____
_____
_____
_____
_____
_____
_____
_____
_____
_____

Prayer...

Lord God,

Thank you for always standing with me. Please help me to do your work and live excellently. Draw me near to you while you bring my Boaz to me. Let me not get weary nor lonely while waiting on the right relationship. Guide me to the right field, God. Let me hear your voice before my feet move. I love you, Lord, and I appreciate you.

Amen.

COMPLETE EXERCISES TWO & THREE ON PAGES 41 & 42

What I'm Gleaning...

Ruth Week 3

Ruth: Week Three.

Read Ruth Chapter 3

Naomi's spirit seems better in this chapter. Perhaps Ruth (who is a Moabite) had inspired Naomi to remember that God is faithful. Sometimes it may take someone who doesn't have as much faith (or the background in Christ) to remind you to have faith. God can use anyone to inspire you to move in the direction He wants you to go. Sometimes, these little reminders from God are subtle and sometimes they are blatant.

I remember when I was in grad school and I would catch the M bus to work. At some point, I always ended up with the same bus driver. Grad school was a new experience for me and while I was going through the transition of being on my own for the first time in life, I managed to keep a smile on my face. Something this bus driver noticed. One day, he complimented my smile. I don't know when it started, but when I would pay for my ticket in the morning, he would slip me a ticket for the ride home. He even started having my ticket home ready to hand to me before I put the money in the machine. I took this kind gesture as what Corie Spieker calls a "God wink." God was letting me know that He has his eye on me. That He sees me. That I should keep going. That He is faithful. God sees you. He sees the pain behind your smile and the faith that makes you smile in spite of the pain. If you listen to His instruction He can and will lead you out of your tough situation. The situation is only tough to you. It is not tough for God. In fact, nothing is too tough for God. That is why He is God.

Naomi instructs Ruth on how to prepare to petition Boaz on becoming a kinsman redeemer. Her instructions include taking a bath, putting on perfume and dressing up (Ruth 3:3). Before you turn your nose up at why she had to do this, realize that men are visual. Also realize that Naomi was not instructing her daughter-in-law to seduce Boaz. She was instructing her to put her best foot forward when making this large request. When you go on a job interview, do you not put on your best? If you want to attract Boaz's proper attention then you will have to pay proper attention to your appearance.

Are you happy with the way you look? If not, what can you do to fix the things that you would like to change and be confident with the things you cannot change?

_____

_____

_____

_____

_____

_____

_____

Another part of Naomi's instruction to Ruth was to lay at Boaz's feet (Ruth 3:4). This should also indicate to you that her appearance was not to seduce Boaz. If that was the case she would have instructed her to lay beside him. But she did not.

Have you ever laid next to someone you shouldn't have? How did it make you feel afterward? What are you going to do differently in your next relationship (I Corinthians 6:18-20)?

_____

_____

_____

_____

_____

_____

When Boaz awoke to find Ruth at his feet, he could have taken advantage of the situation. But he didn't. Because he was Boaz. The man created for Ruth. The kinsman redeemer. He was in her life to redeem not to destroy.

Have you ever had a relationship where the person took advantage of your vulnerability? How did that make you feel? How can you avoid a person like that in your next relationship?

_____

_____

_____

The man that God has for you will not come to destroy you or take you out of the will of God. He will be a perfect gentleman even when there are circumstances that he could take advantage of.

Your Boaz will also speak highly of you (Ruth 3:11). Everyone in the town knew Ruth was a virtuous woman. And Boaz had heard also. Her work and dedication to her mother-in-law, Naomi, spoke wonders.

What would your community/friends say about you (Proverbs 31:28)?

Prayer...

Lord God,

Thank you for your perfect instruction. I pray that you would make me a great listener and that I would hear your voice as you direct me where you want me to go. Help me to put my best foot forward and develop excellence in everything I do. As I am waiting on my Boaz, help me to pay attention to my appearance. Help me to stay Holy in body until you bring me into marriage. Show me anyone who comes into relationship with me only to destroy and not to redeem. Remove them from my path, oh Lord. Guide me toward being a virtuous woman of God. I love you, Lord, and I appreciate you.

Amen.

COMPLETE EXERCISE FOUR ON PAGE 43

What I'm Gleaning...

Ruth: Week Four.

Read Ruth Chapter 4

I'm sure Boaz was elated at the idea of marrying Ruth. He didn't have to be forced at all. Ladies, we can never force anyone to marry us. There is no need to create a Boaz just because you are in a relationship with a man. Boaz will choose you (Proverbs 18:22). And marrying a Ruth isn't easy. You are a valuable woman and your Boaz will go through hoops of fire to make sure you are rightfully his. I'm going to be really honest with you here. In most of my past relationships, I was the pursuer and I pursued hard. If I liked a guy I made it almost impossible for him not to like me or he pretended to like me so I would leave him alone. I tried to create the perfect love in every serious relationship I had because I wanted that romantic, Cinderella story. I wanted to find my prince no matter what. When I was too impatient to find him, I tried to create him. This never worked out. Because the guy wasn't truly invested in loving me. He didn't have to. I made it too easy.

Before Boaz married Ruth he had to petition the closest kinsman redeemer and he also had to do that in front of the elders. Once the nearest kinsman redeemer decided that he could not mess up his own estate by marrying Ruth, Boaz was able to marry her (Ruth 4:6). When you listen to God He will not put you with the wrong man.

Imagine if the other relative had married Ruth. Would we have had Jesus? Your destiny is tied to you being in the right relationships with the people God brings into your life. Because of the relationship between Boaz and Ruth, our savior Jesus Christ was born (Matt. 1:1-16). Hallelujah!

Are you, or have you been in a relationship that you know you were not supposed to be in?

_____

_____

_____

_____

What made you stay in the relationship when you knew it wasn't the right one for you?

_____

_____

_____

_____

_____

_____

_____

Have you ever forced a relationship? Maybe because you thought that you would never find the right one, you tried to fit a round peg in a square hole. What lessons did you learn from that? How can you be sure not to repeat the same mistake?

_____

_____

_____

_____

_____

_____

_____

After reading this study I hope that you will take these lessons from Ruth's life and apply them to your own. I pray that this is your *Get it Right* season and that this study helps you prepare for Boaz by drawing closer to God and away from unhealthy relationships.

Prayer...

Lord God,

Thank you for Ruth and Boaz and the lessons we can learn from their lives. Thank you for preparing me for my Boaz. Thank you that the Boaz you have for me is already excited about me. Thank you that I will not have to force him into a relationship with me. I praise you Lord for creating someone for me who values me, who comes to redeem and not to destroy. Thank you for being the ultimate redeemer and dying for me so that I can have life more abundantly. Thank you for loving me and showing me what it is to be in right relationship. I love you, Lord, and I appreciate you.

Amen.

COMPLETE EXERCISE FIVE ON PAGE 44

What I'm Gleaning...

Exercises 1-5

Exercise One - Growing Covenant Partners

In *Ruth Week One*, we are discussing the importance of being in the right relationship, in this case, with a potential Boaz. But the principle of covenant partnership is the same with friendships as well as romantic relationships. Now that you have listed your covenant partners, it is important to water the seeds of friendship so that these partnerships can grow strong and withstand the test of time. Choose at least one item on the list each week of the study to do with or for your covenant friends. You can also use this list to build other friendships that you want to grow.

- **Send a handwritten card/note.** The power of sending something in the mail is irreplaceable. Your friend will feel loved and appreciated.

- **Ask your friend how you can pray for them.** Praying for your friends is a great way to have a friendship that goes deeper than the surface. Asking them how you can specifically be praying for them shows that you care and are sincerely interested in their cares.

- **Spend Quality Time.** We are so busy texting and communicating via social media that we forget that in-person touch. Make time this week to grab

Exercise One - Growing Covenant Partners cont'd

tea with a friend or call a long distance friend. The power of seeing and hearing is amazing to a friendship.

- **Volunteer together.** Give back to the community while strengthening your friendship and do some volunteer work together.

- **Send them a gift.** Does your friend have a favorite tea? Favorite color? The gift doesn't have to be anything big. Just something that let's them know you are thinking about them and the friendship is important to you.

- **Celebrate God's Grace.** Have you received an answer to prayer? Has your friend? God's word says to rejoice when others are rejoicing (Rom. 12:15). Make time to celebrate the victories God is bringing.

- More tips on thedivainc.com/RuthStudy

We learned in *Ruth Week Two* that Ruth was a worker. She was not concerned with finding a man. She had to take care of her mother-in-law, Naomi. Ruth may have been lonely. I'm sure it is hard to lose your husband and then have to figure out life by yourself, especially in a time where it was critical to have a man to depend on. But the Bible never tells us that she sat around and sulked about it. What it does tell us is that she went to work.

I have many married friends and spending time with them is special. They don't have the luxury of having a spontaneous girls day all the time. They have other responsibilities and many of them have young children. Having this observation of them has helped me to appreciate my singleness more than ever. Because this is the time that I can work on all of the projects God would have me to do without much distraction.

1. In your journal, write down your life dreams for health, wealth, God's Kingdom, career and family.
2. What is God calling you to do in your time of singleness?
3. What parts of your dream have to be accomplished in your singleness?
4. What parts of your dream will you accomplish with your spouse?
5. Write down at least five goals you want to accomplish in the next two years that will help you get closer to the lifestyle you wrote about in #1.
6. Look up verses in the Bible that correspond with the goals you have.

More goal setting tips at thedivainc.com/RuthStudy

Exercise Three - Boaz's Qualities

So you want to get married? I do too. I've always had a list of all of the things I say that I want in my mate. But as I get older and more experienced, I can put the important things into perspective. So let's make a list of what we want vs. the qualities that Boaz has. First, list the qualities that you want in your mate. If you are dating, does your boyfriend have these qualities? Look at past relationships and consider if these qualities were present. Then, go back through the book of Ruth and write down all of the qualities that Boaz had. Do your qualities vs. Boaz's qualities match up? Are there adjustments you need to make?

What I want in my Boaz...

_____
_____
_____
_____
_____
_____
_____
_____
_____
_____
_____
_____

Boaz Qualities according to Ruth

_____
_____
_____
_____
_____
_____
_____
_____
_____
_____
_____

Exercise Four – Paying Appropriate Attention to Your Looks & Health

We had a guest preacher at my church a while back and she asked all the ladies who were believing God for husbands to stand. Awkward! But we all managed to get out of our seats. When we sat back down she taught about the importance of preparing for what you are believing God for. If you want a husband, are you prepared? She asked if we looked the way we wanted to look. There is no reason to wait for the wedding to shed those extra pounds. You can look the way you want to look before he comes. Not just for him, but really for you. It is also important to remember that men are visual. Looking your best, as we discussed in *Ruth Week Three*, is a must. Of course, there will be times where we just don't feel up to it. We are human. But there is a difference between an exception to the rule and the rule.

1. On another sheet of paper or in your journal, write down your goals for your appearance and health before marriage.

2. Write down all the steps you will use to accomplish those goals or make progress in the next year. Is it that you want to eat healthier? What steps can you take now? Do you want to dress better?

3. On a scale of 1-10 (10 being the highest), how important is your physical health and appearance to you?

4. Another important health factor is mental health. What are you doing now, to be mentally healthy for a relationship? Do you feel you are mentally healthy? If not, what are some of the things you plan to do to get your mental health in order?

Want more tips? Head over to thedivainc.com/RuthStudy

Exercise Five – Why I Want to Be Married?

In *Ruth Week Four*, we discussed making sure we are in the right field. And while the field we end up in is truly up to God, if we are listening to Him and letting Him guide our footsteps, we should have an idea of why we want to be married before He leads us there. God will give you the desires of your heart if we delight in Him (Psalm 37:4). So if marriage is what you want, God will give it to you if you are focused on Him. Make a list of the reasons why you want to be married. Then look up what God's Word says about marriage. You can use the rest of this page or a blank sheet in your notebook/journal.

Why I want to be married

_____
_____
_____
_____
_____
_____
_____
_____
_____
_____
_____
_____

What God's word says about marriage

_____
_____
_____
_____
_____
_____
_____
_____
_____
_____
_____
_____

About the author...

Crystal-Marie Mitchell is an Entrepreneur + Writer + Designer + Historical Korean Drama Lover from the Bay Area. She graduated from Florida A&M University with a BS in Graphic Design and received her Master of Arts in Industrial Arts from San Francisco State University.

She is the Owner | Creative Director of IsrylDesigns, a San Francisco based design firm and the Editor-in-Chief of The Diva Inc. Magazine.

Crystal-Marie started The Diva Inc. Magazine as a blog when the economy was rough and she needed an outlet to share her story. Since then, she turned what started as a personal blog into a thriving brand built on encouraging women through tough seasons.

She published her first book in 2015 titled, The Diva Diaries™ Living Through Tough Seasons, where she shares her testimony about her decades long battle with depression, self-esteem and body image and how it began with a simple playground heartbreak.

This is her first devotional of many to come. You can connect with her via social media:

Twitter: @TheDivaDiaries
Instagram: @TheDivaDiaries
Youtube: @TheDivasCircle
Facebook: facebook.com/thedivainc/
Email: info@thedivainc.com

www.ingramcontent.com/pod-product-compliance
Lightning Source LLC
LaVergne TN
LVHW072104070426
835508LV00003B/258